Elliott

Elliott

Brian Muriel

Etchings Press
Indianapolis, Indiana

This publication is made possible by funding provided by the Shaheen College of Arts and Sciences and the Department of English at the University of Indianapolis. Special thanks to the students who judged, edited, designed, and published this chapbook: Abigail Bailey, Rachel Calderone, Riley E. Childers, and Amber Phillips.

UNIVERSITY *of* INDIANAPOLIS

Published by Etchings Press
1400 E. Hanna Ave.
Indianapolis, Indiana 46227
All rights reserved

etchings.uindy.edu
www.uindy.edu/cas/english

Printed by IngramSpark

Published in the United States of America

ISBN 978-1-955521-14-7
28 27 26 25 24   1 2 3 4 5

Cover image by Ryan Moulton
Cover design by Abigail Bailey
Interior design by Abigail Bailey

To my wife.

Table of Contents

"contact"

I see the ground underneath dissolving
as I am given to the sky
it is a rapture of air blasting past
the last weightless moment of a dream
leaking out of memory before my eyes
open to the fresh day of his birth
which was its own phenomenon of flight

and when he came we cried first
then counted his fingers and toes
and announced his name then
brought him home
our world so new
a sequence of curved patterns
(a system of clouds) clustered below

then the static and settling of my stomach
when we came down to meet the ground
all that machinery groaning against the speed
the pitched floor brought back to even
and a boy for us he is ours

(a system of clouds)

a system of clouds drops water
but to see color there must be light
and at my back the sun works to
separate everything into a spectrum
which lengthens my days reflecting
different arcs and angles
and I am told I developed a stammer
it comes and goes

this is the chemical some cortisone
or the amber filling up my textured glass
and once I was someone all out in
front like a period that marks the coming of spring
when fresh life flashes from the window casting
green against all that winter gray
and it is all there propped up to show how cruel it
is to love someone

it is not fair to say it is because of him or try to
maneuver the sun to expose the fragments of
what we lost or never had
it is because my feet float above the ground
and I am thrown from surface to corner as
a sliver of morning light that comes in and divides
my face while I sleep
but it does not wake me it just
fragments my dreams but void
of sensations of sights and real colors
I am lifted and ready

"first crack"

I can mark that moment
when the breach began
and the atmosphere in which
I lived my life tinted to a shade

spinning and slapping his own head
(I pinned the moment down) and squinted my eyes
head cocked to one side
the stuttered heartbeat and
the new knowledge as
the cracks formed in front

and in a blink the years flash behind
and in a moment I am young about six
seeing Elliott hit himself somewhere at a park or party
I make that face the adult me
has seen on other children
the perplexed and nearly maimed
the invasion of space and the strike so sudden
and sharp that the little
mind cannot take it all in at once
on the bouncy bridge but immediately
later buried in her mother's arms on the bench below
she cries because of the quickness of it all
and I cannot apologize
or crinkle my brow or make
my voice tinny because I am also a child stunned

and I am now myself
or the me from years ago
and in that room among
the mylar balloons and a pink and green cake sheathed in
plastic that pops when opened and he is there
my little piercing top
hitting his own head in motion

(I pinned the moment down)

I pinned the moment down
and squinted my eyes in
the same way yarn is tangled
into something useful or forgotten
the hook and its intertwinement
the stitch of daylight sucked out
of space and working to make
the twisted strains of fiber
something whole

it is coming and going that I love
the arriving and leaving
and when you stand back and say you
made this be it a scarf or a child there is
always a bending of the universe
taking the energy and repurposing it into
something one can touch
this is how to love someone completely

"giving your son a name"

we gave our son a name and in those early days it fit
we embroidered it on pillows or stenciled it on pastel walls
and stood back from across the room and imagined the letters
emblazoned on diplomas or etched in the cardstock of invitations

but then the weeks started to unfold slowly
and (the length of a year) became an outer space
with all its collapsing stars and churning nebula
and we began to think the name ill fits
he should have been called something else

and maybe the messages home
from the school would be less of a jolt if
his name was something else
would children flee from him if we
changed what we gave him
would he have been born this way under a new name
maybe naming him before he came casted a straight a crack that
left all of us separated to one side submerged together
in a colloid where our particles do not settle in any given atmosphere

here and now no amount of makeshift names
can undo this fog that is clouding our eyes
it permeates then collects at
the sides of sight and makes its way in
there is nothing left to second guess
especially his name
together we are suspended
in a cloud passing overhead looking down at rivers
and schoolyards and the outsides of homes
high above try to catch then force the symbols into spaces
make them letters so we can rename him

(the length of a year)

the length of a year collects
in the stretch of skin
and amidst all of this
we try and manage again
to bring new life

when we told our sons and
saw their faces my mind eventually went
to names and identities
and how rivers find confluences
and eventually collect and overcome the earth

how do I choose what to multiply
which patterns to build or layout
in front to force me to face the day
and all its rocks jutting out splitting
water for just a moment

it is a feat that I see so much
good in something new and
even think it could save me

"city on a rooftop"

an edge becomes an angle only
when it is noticed
and side by side it takes my breath
away to see the differences unfolding
year after year

it is a parallel it is a path
it is a chart or a graph
a mark on a line
(that we can place) and
say why is it this way for us

to bring the point to the then and there

once in the city high on a rooftop
I was told something
by a friend about his own son
and I imagined myself
being suddenly vertical
passing so straightly the windows
the speed of the air
and the street

(that we can place)

that we can place
in a moment collected and reseen
he points at the camera and enunciates
each syllable so effortlessly
I can remember thinking there he is a
a perfect boy

his eyes move from the camera
to mine off screen and with
a single finger elongated
upright he says
daddy again and sends
these images into an aperture
a fixed space to reanimate
a moment for us when
we need to be reminded
that he was once a child
plastered in yogurt
being captured by young parents
balancing our lives on his words

"four lungs"

when he is a harm to himself and in heaps
or found from outside halfway hanging
from his window
I lay him down on the beige carpet
of his room and press my body flat to his
our rib cages tectonic plates our
four lungs an archipelago

we started this when he
was four and beside himself
a dangerous boy

we could not leave him up there alone like this

I added the breaths when he was six
when (just my weight was not enough)
he knows to receive my breath
to bring it down and
return it to me and this
goes on until he is stopped and fully grounded

at eight he became half my weight
I grip the floor to press more
of myself than I have into him but it is not
enough so I rise like some sort
of Atlas ashamed and aged

(just my weight was not enough)

just my weight was not enough
to stop the oven of my head
churning to warm
taking in gas from tubes
connected to outside lines and
clicking as it does
being tired and slow to fire

the hoping is a sort of living
a soft shine off a new coat of
paint holding light that
spills in from the looseness of a curtain

the question comes
I often wondered how much of my
own atoms need to mingle for me
to swirl in an atmosphere
before I disappear
it is so much unfolding and
folding living this way
a sense of being swallowed
or sided

"his brother"

his brother tethered to him two years apart
they are two clocks hung to the wall
like perfect lovers with the
same energy source
identical nail anchored into the same vertical post
the same first beats
of the first morning

then after time a subtle
graze of the mechanism that
makes the parts move puts
a microsecond between the two times
so they stutter and the perfect rhythm is gone
it breaks the heart to see
the painstaking synchronization stopped

there he is watching his brother get married
there he is entering his brother's first home
I can see it standing on the face of a clock looking up
as the hand sweeps overhead

we are always questioned when we started to know
it is the same as being asked what
made the one mainspring
force the movement delay
I can say when his brother
set off into the grass (and
fell seamlessly into orbit) and
his older brother in the stunted
shade of a tree counting seconds alone
the two timepieces on a wall in our home
each forever on their own plane

(and fell seamlessly into orbit)

and fell seamlessly into orbit
the slow spin of matter or
the twisting of chromosomes
to form a body
at three times you were not alone
inside yourself and now outward
they are here growing
the same tinge of skin
the same patterns
in their hair the same
shaping of the small words
to cover the gaps

looking at them what you carried
I think about the even trees that line our street
how the leaves flutter in unison
at even heights
all those leftover stunted limbs
clipped down for their differences
as if love could be pruned
by ignoring that question
I am too ashamed to ask anyone
am I good
am I good

"dream"

I woke in the haze of night and upon realizing
the past sequence was just a dream I decided I wanted to die
the idea to leave came so honestly that (it almost
slowed my heart to a stop) but I
stayed and lifted my body from the bed

the dream I had was we ran to a cave and talked
it was him but not him
no odd cadence in his voice
no stimming about the height
of the poles outside our house

he was normal

we talked plainly about girls he
thought about and his
friends and the insides of their homes
in this dream I was the father I always
wanted to be and then I woke up

(it almost slowed my heart to a stop)

it almost slowed my heart to a stop
when in the late winter
the only time we could
see him was on a screen
draped in a fabric we did not give him
all corners and backlighting and
how he floated in and out of view
I made my voice jingle for my son
I made my eyes bright to play interference
between the realness and what he
thought was happening to him

those days when he was there was a sort
of parallel or concurrence
so much quiet and stillness bound to
the tantrum happening inside us all
he tried new foods and lived in the city
and we broke down and made it all orderly
aligning our home while he was gone

after a time the house seemed stale from the void of
of the slamming of sheetrock
the kicking of doors
and the haphazard expansion of rapidly heated
air crashing into all of us day in and out
but that last night when enough became enough
the only remnant of noise
was the siren taking him away

and there was something
about his mother my bride being
allowed to dress him for bed when he came
there that first late night that emptied all I had left

"an arm's reach"

an arm's reach
from him means there
is no time
to subtract space
and lunge or block my
body between his

as such unguarded high drops or
steepness beside our steps
forces my hand to
graze the backside fabric
of his shirt when
we are single file
and walking straight

the span of my limbs is all I have
to prevent such a shattering
of a commonplace
Sunday or a father's day picnic

what a way to live

and there is always some deafening
compressor or siren or backfire
that chop my hands to his ears

looking back at that first
afternoon when the
earliest crack came and
he only a small child slapping his
own head so much for us
to not know

(we are a sight)
the two of us standing on a blue plastic bridge
or posted together looking down a curved slide
I always go first
waiting to catch him at the bottom

(we are a sight)

we are a sight
can you see us
under a night sky that is
bursting with color and sound
I became God in the grass

my hands cupping
my son's ears as I knelt
behind his young body
so many moments spent this way
hands pressed to ears
hands gripping wrists
gatherings I have missed or games spent sidelined
he and I always
together and alone but in the grass among the cacophony
of pops and murmurs
I feel the miracle of magic embedded
in my veins and into hands
pressed tightly on the sides of a small face
this is what God feels like
when he forces
the pain of creation to a yield giving
a moment when I exist
only for him

does my child know that a body is connected to
these hands
a back tightened
from fatigue and knees ground past the grass
and into the dirt
does it matter to him or does he not
notice the full weight of these
bones and everything else inside
directing the energy to these hands
and so the explosions in the sky
that are simultaneous with their
light but carry sound slowly behind
are blocked by my palms and barely make
their way into him

craned up to the sky he sees the
streaks burst upward and then bloom reds and blues and
greens and then rain down shards
of light before fizzling to black
and his lips curled up once and he clapped
having his own hands freed from his ears

"this puncturing and this pain"

my son's teeth sinking into my skin is a gift
breaking the surface
I want him deeper until
my arm is in pieces devoured and gone
the sharp intake of air that comes a moment after
the moment of submission
being brought down to my knees
within the environment
then beneath it
such a spectacle we are thrashing
around the staff bathroom of this haircut place
our love is never transactional

I did not know I needed this pain
until the electricity in his mouth met my body
and now as I look down at his little face
so striking in its contortions
I feel the miracle of real pain
this puncturing and this pain leaves
a mark to be seen and hopefully a scar
it is so much easier to wear him this way
this violent display that is heard by
strangers waiting for a blowout or a dye

the latch clicks open and we emerge
and I pretend that I am asked about
the small indentations on my arm
how they got there but at the last moment I lie
(keeping this beautiful secret just for me)
a trophy
a letter
an outward gleaming
testament of my love

(keeping this beautiful secret just for me)

keeping this beautiful
secret just for me:

sometimes he sashays
through the living room
stimming about numbers
if he gets overly excited about
a measurement
or a weight or a
linear sequence of some kind
he will hop twice
twist his wrists
and smile

in that microsecond
when his feet are
off the ground and
he is ranting about the
height of our dog
or the size of the celery
I will see him joyful
I seep inside all that bright light
where there are no differences
or comparisons
or forebodings
within that flash of air between
his feet and floor
there is just lightness
that crashes through sending me out of the room
to where I see my life glinting in the
sunlight that breaks the surface
of water.

About Etchings Press

Etchings Press is a student-run publisher at the University of Indianapolis that runs a post-publication award—the Whirling Prize—as well as an annual publication contest for one poetry chapbook, one prose chapbook, and one novella. On occasion, Etchings Press publishes new chapbooks from previous winners. For more information about these contests and the Whirling Prize post-publication award, please visit etchings.uindy.edu.

Poetry
2024: *Elliott* by Brian Muriel
2023: *Other Side of Sea* by Xiaoqiu Qiu
2022: *A Place That Knows You* by Tiwaladeoluwa Adekunle
2022: *The Vaudeville Horse* by Elizabeth Kerlikowske
2021: *My Mother's Ghost Scrubs the Floor at 2 a.m.* by Robert Okaji
2020: *Vaginas Need Air* by Tori Grant Welhouse
2019: *As Lovers Always Do* by Marne Wilson
2018: *In the Herald of Improbable Misfortunes* by Robert Campbell
2017: *Uncle Harold's Maxwell House Haggadah* by Danny Caine
2016: *Some Animals* by Kelli Allen
2015: *Velocity of Slugs* by Joey Connelly
2014: *Action at a Distance* by Christopher Petruccelli

Prose
2024: *We Obedient Children* by Karris Rae (fiction and nonfiction hybrid)
2023: *Leaving the House Unlocked* by Elizabeth Enochs (nonfiction)
2022: *Triple Point* by Laura Story Johnson (essays)
2021: *Bad Man Love Stories* by Curtis VanDonkelaar (fiction)
2020: *Three in the Morning and You Don't Smoke Anymore* by Peter J. Stavros (fiction)

2019: *Dissenting Opinion from the Committee for the Beatitudes* by Marc J. Sheehan (fiction)

2018: *The Forsaken* by Chad V. Broughman (fiction)

2017: *Unravelings* by Sarah Cheshire (memoir)

2016: *Pathetic* by Shannon McLeod (essays)

2015: *Ologies* by Chelsea Biondolillo (essays)

2014: *Static: Stories* by Frederick Pelzer (fiction)

Novella

2024: *Pineville Trace* by Wes Blake

2023: *Our Cadaver* by Elizabeth Toman

2022: *Goodbye to the Ocean* by Susan L. Lin

2021: *Miss Alma May Learns to Fight* by Stuart Rose

2020: *Under Black Leaves* by Doug Ramspeck

2019: *Savonne, Not Vonny* by Robin Lee Lovelace

2018: *Edge of the Known Bus Line* by James R. Gapinski

2017: *The Denialist's Almanac of American Plague and Pestilence* by Christopher Mohar

2016: *Followers* by Adam Fleming Petty

Chapbooks from Previous Winners

2022: *slighted…* by Chad V. Broughman (fiction)

2020: *Fruit Rot* by James R. Gapinski (fiction)

2016: *#LOVESONG* by Chelsea Biondolillo (microessays with photos and found text)

Brian Muriel is a high school English teacher and poet from Naperville, Illinois, where he lives with his wife and young family. His work has appeared in *West Trade Review*, *La Piccioletta Barca*, *The Ekphrastic Review*, and others.

www.ingramcontent.com/pod-product-compliance
Lightning Source LLC
Chambersburg PA
CBHW051651120626
46551CB00015B/2314

Endorsements for *Pray for Him*

Pray for Him is a wonderful resource! I appreciate the practical and scriptural examples of specific areas in which to pray for my pastor-husband. During seasons of his ministry, I have taken a page a day through my daily prayer time to prompt current avenues of prayer. I have also taken copies of *Pray for Him* on missions trips to share with missionaries and national pastors' wives. It is a relevant resource in any culture! Our present ministry allows me to interact weekly with pastors' wives across our state. Many of them have benefited from *Pray for Him*, and I look forward to sharing it with new pastors' wives as they engage in this crucial ministry of intercession for their husbands.

Robin Jones
Wife of Scott Jones, State Missions Director, Wisconsin Fellowship of Baptist Churches

———————

As a Christian, I've been challenged to pray Scripture. Faith Taylor has compiled Scripture passages in a clear and succinct format, making it easy to pray biblically for my pastor-husband. I've used this tool regularly and passed this booklet on to other pastors' wives. It is a great help to my prayer life.

Heidi Fernett
Wife of Brian Fernett, Senior Pastor, First Baptist Church, Lebanon, Pennsylvania

More than anyone except God, a ministry wife knows what her husband is facing. Maybe nobody else knows. Maybe no one else is praying. There is power in a wife's prayers when they are grounded in Scripture and passionate for God's glory. This booklet helps me keep my focus on God's goals for my husband as I pray for him. I know it will help you, too.

Claudia Barba
Wife of Dave Barba, Press On! Ministries

Pray for Him sits on my side table, where I read my Bible and pray. The compilation of prayers helps me pray informed, biblically-based prayers for my pastor-husband. I know my Father desires to answer these prayers since I am praying His words back to Him. I found the book so helpful that I have begun handing it out to other pastors' wives who want to pray better for their pastor-husbands.

Beneth Perry
Wife of Ron Perry, Faith Baptist Church, Folsom, California